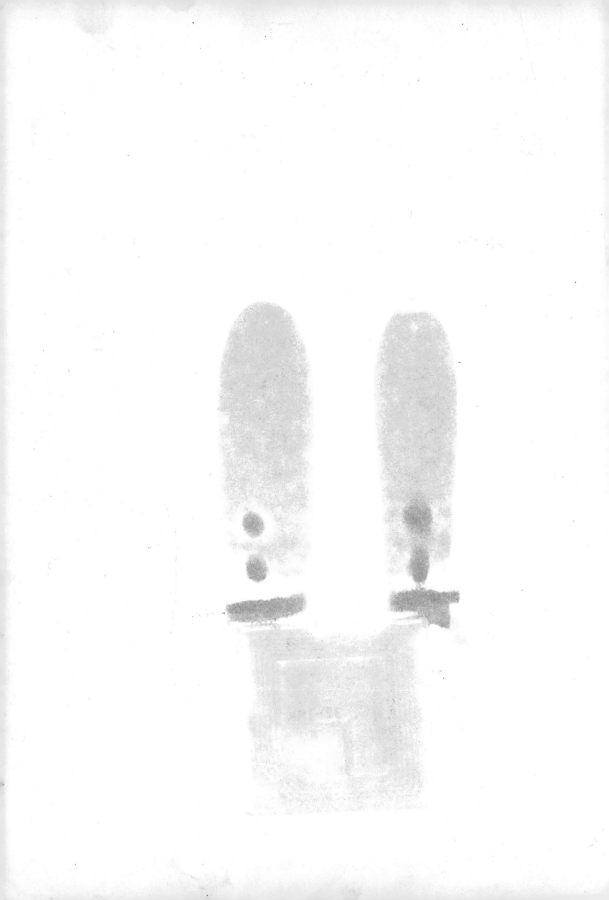

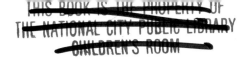

Where Animals Live

The World of Dragonflies

Words by Virginia Harrison

Adapted from Christopher O'Toole's
The Dragonfly over the Water

Photographs by
Oxford Scientific Films

Gareth Stevens Publishing
Milwaukee

Contents

Dragonflies and Where They Live

If you are near a weedy pond or slow river during the summer, you will probably find dragonflies.

There are many *species* of dragonfly, about 5,000 in the world, and many have lots of bright colors.

Water is very important to them because their *larvae* mature there. Like the adults, larvae are *predators* of insects and other underwater *prey*.

Although water is their main *habitat*, many large species can be seen hunting insects on forest trails.

The Dragonfly's Body

Dragonflies have three body regions, as do most insects: the head, *thorax*, and *abdomen*.

The thorax has two pairs of wings and three pairs of legs.

The long, thin abdomen has ten *segments* and contains the gut and the sex organs.

A relative of the dragonfly is the more slender damselfly. Alike in their prey and coloring, the damselflies have the same body parts.

Dragonflies perch with their wings spread out (above), while damselflies fold their wings over their bodies.

The dragonfly has an outside skin which acts as a skeleton, called an *exoskeleton*. It is a waterproof substance called chitin, and all of the muscles are attached to it. The skin has pores, called *spiracles*, through which insects breathe.

Dragonflies have a glow to their skin, creating vivid colors and delicate patterns. The glow can be waxy or metallic.

The wings of the dragonfly are made of many veins that make them rigid and strong.

The Dragonfly's Head

The dragonfly's large, often connected *eyes* cover most of its head. The damselfly also has large eyes, but they are separated.

The eyes are very sensitive to movement, which is important to the dragonfly's survival. With them, dragonflies can escape from enemies, detect prey, and find mates.

Dragonflies' eyes are called *compound* because each is made up of thousands of tiny *facets*.

↑

Other features on the head are the *antennae* and jaws. The antennae are two feelers between the eyes. They help the damselfly or dragonfly guide itself.

The jaws each have several cutting teeth that crunch up insects.

The whole head is attached to a narrow neck and helps to balance the dragonfly as it flies.

Hunting on the Wing

Dragonflies breed near water, but they can often be found in forest clearings hunting for insects. Some adults hunt in deserts, far from water.

If we watch dragonflies carefully, we can see that there are two ways in which they fly. A larger "hawker" swoops upward as it flies to catch an insect. A smaller "darter" sits on a perch, darts up to catch an insect, and returns to the same perch.

Dragonflies attack their prey from below. Their eyes are made so that the facets on the top see movement while the facets on the bottom see still objects.

Dragonflies can fly very quickly. They can reach speeds of 15-21 mph (25-35 kph). One species from Australia has been clocked at 35 mph (57 kph)! Dragonflies fly skillfully, too. They can fly backward, loop the loop, and hover.

Dragonflies are skilled aerial hunters. When a dragonfly catches an insect, it uses its six legs as a cage to grasp it and pass it to the mouth. It does all this much faster than it takes you to read about it!

Dragonflies and damselflies are unique insects because their wings can beat independently of one another. The thorax is tilted backwards and contains large and strong flight muscles. This gives the thorax a powerful appearance.

Damselflies hunt nearer to water than dragonflies. Large numbers of dragonflies often "swarm feed," or eat in large groups.

Dragonflies also follow people and animals through the brush in Africa to feed on the insects that have been disturbed.

Dragonflies and damselflies also sometimes feed on each other, just as this damselfly is eating another it has caught.

⬇

Temperature Control: Warming Up and Cooling Down

Like all insects, dragonflies and damselflies are cold-blooded when inactive. They get their warmth from the sun. Each morning, they must sunbathe until they are warm enough to fly.

Another way dragonflies warm up is by rapidly shivering their wing muscles.

Sometimes dragonflies absorb heat from warm objects. A sun-warmed log provides heat for this dragonfly.

If the air is hot and the dragonfly is active, it may need to cool down. Large dragonflies cool their blood by letting it circulate through their bodies. Or they cool off by gliding through the air without moving their wings.

If they can't find shade, dragonflies point their bodies straight up, so that the sun is hitting less of the surface area.

Courtship and Territory

Hot, sunny days are the best time to watch dragonfly courtship and mating.

Some males simply try to grab the nearest passing female — or even another male — to mate with. But most dragonflies have special rituals they perform. Females can then identify the male as a member of their species. Patterned wings aid in identification.

This male is guarding its *territory* from a branch. Males set up territories and defend them against rival males. The size and location of the territory depends upon the species.

Many dragonfly species use some sort of special dance flight in courting to put the females into a trance. Others dangle their patterned legs to lure the female into their territory.

↑

Mating

Before two dragonflies or damselflies mate, they fly or perch in the "tandem" position, as these damselflies are doing.

The actual mating position is somewhat different for the damselfly and dragonfly, however. Both use the "wheel" position, and the male uses *claspers* at the end of his abdomen to grasp the female. The male damselfly grasps the female by the front of her thorax.

↓

The male dragonfly grasps the female by her head.

Before the male dragonfly or damselfly mates, he competes to be the last one to deposit the *sperm* that will fertilize the female's eggs. This competition ensures that he will be the father of the next generation.

Egg Laying

The female dragonfly usually lays her eggs soon after mating. She dips the tip of her abdomen below the water and releases the eggs.

Often, the male stays nearby to keep any rival males away. He wants to make sure she does not mate again.

Some species deposit their eggs directly into the water. Those eggs are usually round. Others lay their eggs in water plants or water-logged tree stumps. These eggs are usually oblong.

↑

The damselfly male almost always stays with his mate while she lays eggs. Sometimes they even stay attached.

The female lays the eggs through a tube at the end of the abdomen. This tube may be small for laying eggs underwater. Or it may be curved, like a blade, for cutting a slit in a plant for the eggs.

If the female is totally underwater when laying her eggs, she covers herself in an air bubble.

↓

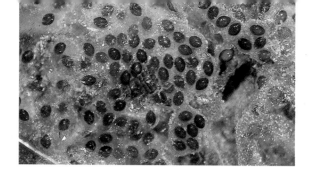

Growing Up Under Water

Dragonfly eggs settle on leaves under water until they hatch into larvae. The larvae, or nymphs, do not yet have the ability to fly, nor the brilliant colors of the adult.

Damselfly larvae are long and thin with three leaf-like gills at the end of the abdomen. They use the gills like flippers as they swim in their side-to-side motion.

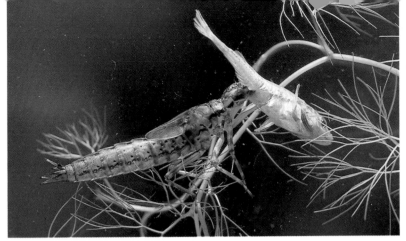

All larvae creep through the mucky bottoms of lakes and among the water plants. Larvae are predators of many small water creatures, including small fish. The larvae have a unique jaw, called a "mask," that spears its prey in an instant (see picture below).

Larvae grow into adult dragonflies after a series of *molts* in which the nymph increases in size. After the fourth molt, wings begin to develop. The larval stage of the dragonfly can last from 100 days to 2-5 years. This larva is molting its skin.

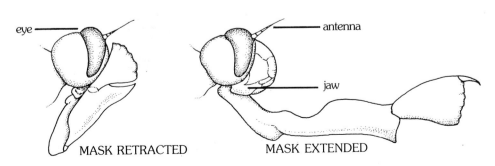

eye ——— ——— antenna

——— jaw

MASK RETRACTED   MASK EXTENDED

The mask of the dragonfly larva

Emergence

Before dragonflies and damselflies emerge from the water, they must find a way to climb out, such as a reed or stem.

The country's climate determines whether the larva emerges during the day or night. It needs warmth when it leaves the water. Once out, the dragonfly pulls itself out of its larval skin.

The larva sits motionless for about 45 minutes, until the old skin cracks. Blood pumps through the bodies of both the dragon- and damselfly larvae. The wings dry and expand. The cuticle skin dries and hardens.

The dragonfly hangs its head down a while before completely emerging. The majority of its life is over, for the adult lives only about a month.

The newly emerged adult sits on its cast-off skin, while its new skin hardens and darkens and begins to lay down its color pattern.

23

Dragonflies Around the World

There is a total of 5,000 species of dragonflies and damselflies around the world. Some of them have unusual lives and sizes.

This South American damselfly larva feeds on mosquito larvae.

The tropical forest of South America is the home of this damselfly. It is the largest species in the world, with wingspans of up to 7 inches (18 cm). It flies by night, stealing insects caught in spiders' webs.

There are some strange larvae, too. Some no longer live in water at all, and some live in torrential waterfalls. That species, an African dragonfly, clings to the stones. The adults fly in the waterfall spray zone.

↑

Enemies

There is a wide range of enemies for all stages of the dragonfly. This dragonfly is being eaten by a spider after getting caught in its web.

Several kinds of parasitic wasps pierce the dragonfly eggs and lay their own inside. But for larvae, the greatest enemies are fish, waterbugs, and ducks. And if overcrowding occurs, the larvae will even eat each other.

Larvae have ways of diguising themselves in the muck, but the newly emerged adults are defenseless until their wings have dried. They may be eaten by birds and other larger dragonflies. Other threats to an adult dragonfly include swallows, herons, and ducks. Fish will eat egg-laying females.

This dragonfly has been trapped in a sundew plant. The plant has special juices to digest insects.

Dragonflies and People

People have responded to dragonflies in many different ways. Some people have thought of dragonflies as mysterious and evil. But they are harmless, even helpful, to people. In some places, dragonflies actually catch horseflies that swarm near horses. In this way they help rather than harm the horses.

In some countries, dragonflies are eaten. In Indonesia, they are served in a curried soup with tadpoles and small fish. In Malaysia, dragonflies are fried with onions.

Ancient Chinese art portrays beautiful images of dragonflies. Japan also celebrates the dragonfly in poetry and art. And both China and Japan value dragonflies for their medicinal powers. The dragonfly is also said to have spiritual powers.

The drainage of this pond has ruined a habitat for many species of plants, fish, and insects. Perhaps we are more dangerous to dragonflies than they are to us.

Life Around Water

Dragonflies and damselflies are at the center of a web of relationships between animals. They eat small animals, and they in turn are eaten by larger ones. Here is a diagram to outline the food chains.

Food Chain

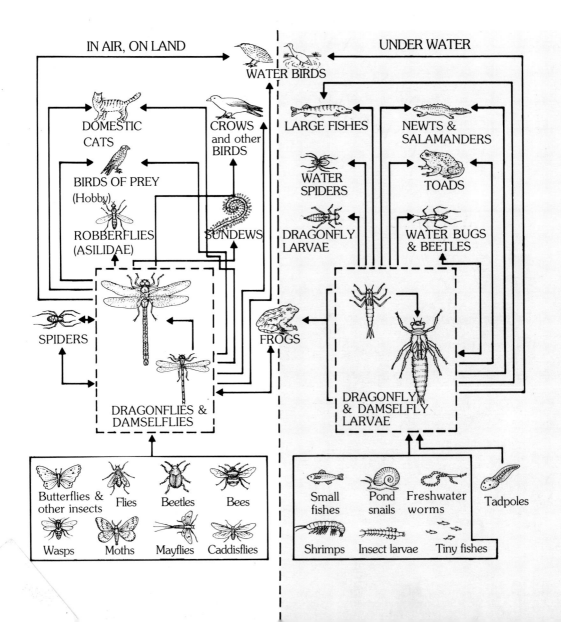

In addition to ponds and food, dragon- and damselflies need plenty of vegetation in their habitat.

Despite surpluses of grain, some farmers are paid to drain ponds and fill in the spaces to grow more. The loss of habitat, along with pollution, is harmful to the dragonfly's way of life.

People can do much to help the dragonfly. Preserving and creating ponds can make a new home for insects and other wildlife, too.

Index and New Words About Dragonflies

These new words about dragonflies appear in the text on the pages shown after each definition. Each new word first appears in the text in *italics*, just as it appears here.

abdomen ......the rear of the three body parts of an insect, containing the gut and sex organs . **4, 16, 18, 19, 20**

antennae ......feelers on the head that contain the sense of touch and, possibly, hearing and smell. **7**

claspers ....a pair of hinged, finger-like structures at the end of a male dragonfly's abdomen that are used to grasp the female. **16**

compound eye ....an eye made up of thousands of facets, each with its own lens and connection to the brain. **6**

exoskeleton ...the horny, outer shell of insects, which encloses and protects the soft parts and to which the muscles are attached. **5**

facet ....one of the thousands of units that make up a compound eye. **6, 9**

habitat ....the natural home of any animal or plant. **3, 29, 31**

larva ....(plural larvae) the form of an insect that emerges from the egg. **3, 20, 21, 22, 23, 24, 25, 26, 27**

mask ....the hinged lower lip used to catch prey and found only in the larvae of dragonflies and damselflies. **21**

molt ....to cast off an old skin or shell. **21**

predator ....an animal that kills and eats other animals. **3, 21**

prey ....an animal that is hunted and killed by another animal for food. **3, 4, 6, 9, 21**

segment ....one of several similar parts forming the body or part of the body of an insect. **4**

species ....a type of animal (or plant) that can interbreed successfully with others of its kind, but not with those of a different type. **3, 9, 14,15, 18, 24, 25, 29**

sperm ....(short for spermatozoa): male sex cells that fertilize the eggs of the female. **17**

spiracles ....breathing holes in insects, each connecting with a fine network of tubes, taking oxygen to all parts of the body. **5**

territory ....an area defended by a male for mating or feeding purposes. **14, 15**

thorax ....the middle of the three body parts of an insect, containing the flight muscles and bearing the wings and six legs. **4, 10, 16**

Reading level analysis: SPACHE 3.5, FRY 3-4, FLESCH 80 (very easy), RAYGOR 3-4, FOG 5, SMOG 3

Library of Congress Cataloging-in-Publication Data

Virginia Harrison, 1966-   The world of dragonflies.   (Where animals live)   Adaptation of: The dragonfly over the water.   Includes index.
Summary: Simple text and photographs depict dragonflies feeding, breeding, and defending themselves in their natural habitats.
1. Dragonflies—Juvenile literature. [1. Dragonflies] I. O'Toole, Christopher. Dragonfly over the water. II. Oxford Scientific Films. III. Title. IV. Series.   QL520.H37 1988   595.7'33   87-42610
ISBN 1-55532-335-9   ISBN 1-55532-310-3 (lib. bdg.)
North American edition first published in 1988 by
Gareth Stevens, Inc.   7317 West Green Tree Road Milwaukee, WI 53223, USA
US edition, this format, copyright © 1988 by Belitha Press Ltd.   Text copyright © 1988 by Gareth Stevens, Inc.
All rights reserved. No part of this book may be reproduced in any form or by any means without permission in writing from Gareth Stevens, Inc.
First conceived, designed, and produced by Belitha Press Ltd., London, as **The Dragonfly over the Water**, with an original text copyright by Oxford Scientific Films. Format copyright by Belitha Press Ltd.
Printed in Hong Kong by South China Printing Co.   Typeset in Milwaukee by Web Tech, Inc.
Series Editor: Mark J. Sachner.   Art Director: Treld Bicknell.   Design: Naomi Games.
Cover Design: Gary Moseley.   Line Drawings: Lorna Turpin.   Scientific Consultant: Gwynne Vevers.
The publishers wish to thank the following for permission to reproduce copyright material:
Oxford Scientific Films Ltd. for title page, pp. 5 below, 7, 14 above, 15, 17 above, 19 both, 20 all, 22 both, 23 both, 25, front and back cover (G.I. Bernard); p. 2 (Gerald Thompson); pp. 3 and 18 above (Bob Frederick); pp. 4 above, 10, 12 above, 13, 16 below, and 17 below (Alistair Shay); p. 4 below (Peter Gathercole); pp. 5 above, 16 above, 18 below, and 26 (Tom Leach); p. 6 (Nick Woods); p. 9 (Sean Morris); p. 11 above (M.F. Black); p. 12 below (D.J. Stradling); pp. 14 below and 27 (Patti Murray); p. 21 (Stephen Dalton); p. 24 (J.A.L. Cooke); p. 28 (David and Sue Cayless); p. 31 E.R. Degginger); Prema Photos for p. 11 above (K.G. Preston). P. 29 is © 1987 The Detroit Institute of Fine Arts, General Membership and Donations Fund.